THE HOT AIR BALLOON RACE

BY RACHEL BACH

AMICUS READERS 1 AMICUS INK

Say Hello to Amicus Readers.

You'll find our helpful dog, Amicus, chasing a ball—to let you know the reading level of a book.

1

Learn to Read

High frequency words and close photo-text matches introduce familiar topics and provide ample support for brand new readers.

2

Read Independently

Some repetition is mixed with varied sentence structures and a select amount of new vocabulary words are introduced with text and photo support.

3

Read to Know More

Interesting facts and engaging art and photos give fluent readers fun books both for reading practice and to learn about new topics.

Amicus Readers and Amicus Ink are imprints of Amicus
P.O. Box 1329, Mankato, MN 56002
www.amicuspublishing.us

Editor: Wendy Dieker
Designer: Tracy Myers
Photo Researchers: Derek Brown and Aubrey Harper

Library of Congress Cataloging-in-Publication Data
Names: Bach, Rachel, author.
Title: The hot air balloon race / by Rachel Bach.
Description: Mankato, Minnesota : Amicus, [2017] | Series: Let's race
Identifiers: LCCN 2015041495 (print) | LCCN 2015049329 (ebook) | ISBN
  9781607539148 (library binding) | ISBN 9781681510385 (eBook) | ISBN
  9781681521336 (paperback)
Subjects: LCSH: Ballooning--Juvenile literature.
Classification: LCC GV762 .B34 2017 (print) | LCC GV762 (ebook)
  | DDC 797.5/1--dc23
LC record available at http://lccn.loc.gov/2015041495

Photo Credits: Feverpitched/iStock cover; vkbhat/iStock 3; davelogan/iStock 4; Avid Creative, Inc./iStock 6-7; Michael Cavazos/Associated Press 8; MariuszBlach/iStock 10-11; Southwest UK Imaging/Alamy Stock Photo 12; Paul D deBerjeois/colorbandit.com 15; huronphoto/iStock 16

Printed in the United States of America.

HC 10 9 8 7 6 5 4 3 2 1
PB 10 9 8 7 6 5 4 3 2 1

Dad takes us to the balloon race.

People get ready for the race.

Derek pulls the gas burner.

Hot air goes in.

The balloons go
up, up, up!

One pilot sets the target. It is a big X.

Ten balloons go. Will they find the X?

The wind blows.

The pilots work hard.

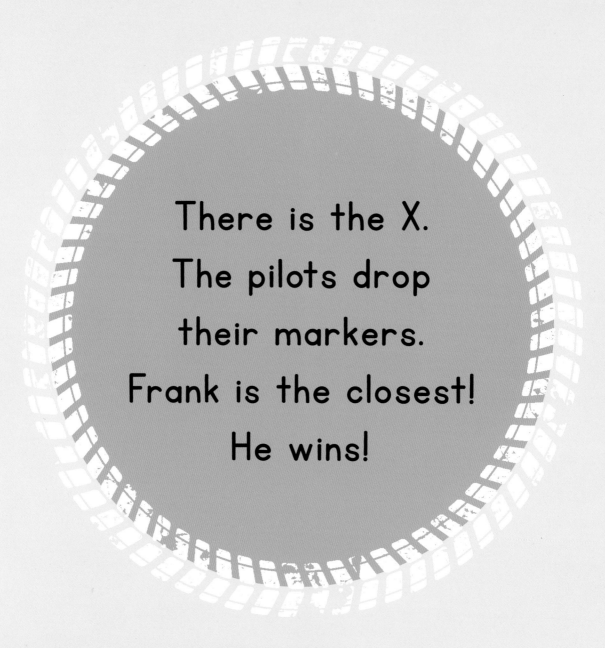

There is the X.
The pilots drop
their markers.
Frank is the closest!
He wins!

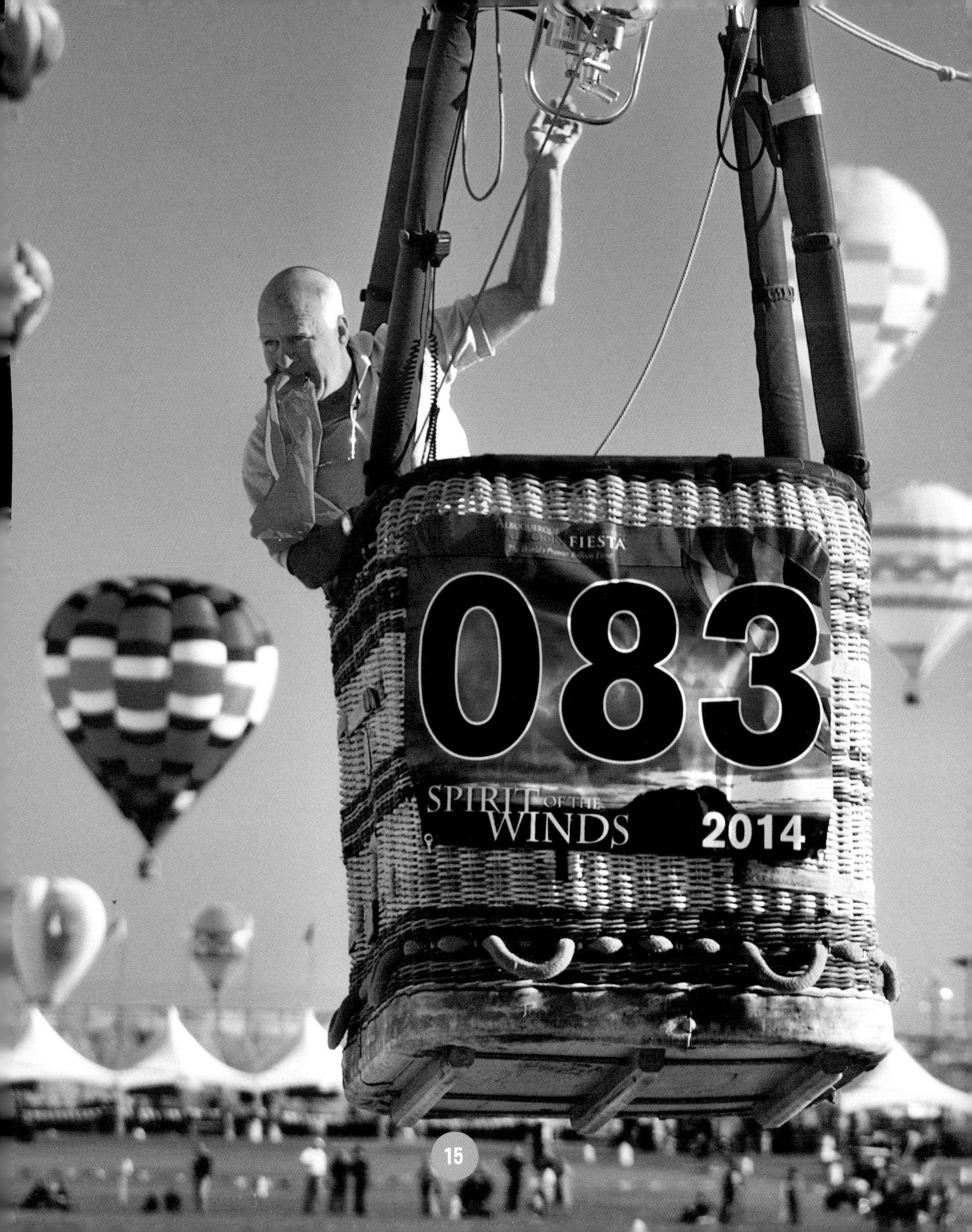
083
SPIRIT OF THE WINDS
2014

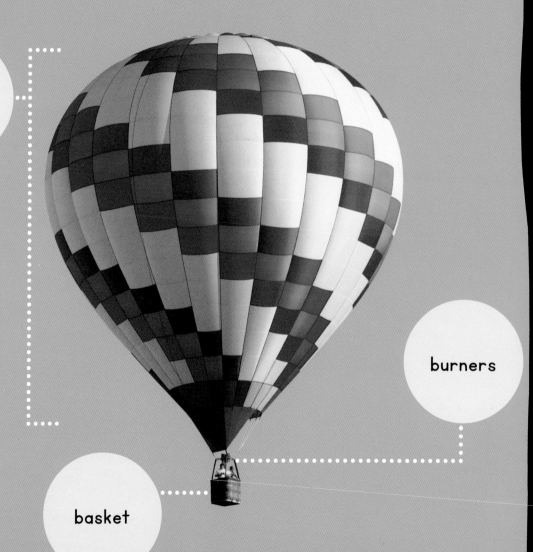

envelope

burners

basket